The Christmas Story

A True History of the Holidays

by Matthew Bowers

Part of the *Free to Think Series* of Educational Supplements

THE CHRISTMAS STORY:
A TRUE HISTORY OF THE HOLIDAYS

Part of the *Free to Think Series* of Educational Supplements

Published by
Travelers Series Publishing, LLC
11858 Bernardo Plaza Court
Suite 230
San Diego, CA 92128.

Written by Matthew Bowers. Copyright © 2012. All rights reserved. No part of this publication may be reproduced, stored or transmitted by any means or in any forms including electronic, photocopying, mechanical, scanning, recording or otherwise without prior written consent of the copyright holder. Requests and inquiries should be addressed in writing to the publisher at Travelers Series Publishing, Inc., 11858 Bernardo Plaza Court, Suite 230, San Diego, CA 92128

For Micaela and Jacob.
Never stop asking questions.

The Christmas Story

What is the Christmas story? There is no easy answer.

To Christians, the story of Christmas is about the birth of Jesus Christ. The word "Christmas" literally means "Christ's Mass," and it commemorates the Christian belief that God sent his only son to live among humans.

But Christmas is much older than Christianity. In fact, Christianity isn't even the first religion to observe a god's birthday on December 25. Romans celebrated the birth of the Persian god Mithras on December 25, as did believers of more than a dozen other gods throughout history. As a result, many of America's most cherished holiday traditions have little to do with Jesus. Christmas trees, gift exchanges, caroling, lights, reindeer, Santa Claus and many other traditions are based on pagan or ancestral beliefs that are thousands of years old. The true story of Christmas is as

Humans have held celebrations in the last week of December throughout recorded and archeological history. Ancient civilizations and priests recognized winter solstice, the shortest day of the year, as an important transition from lifeless winter to spring's new life. As time passed, important festivals grew up around winter solstice, such as Saturnalia in the south of Europe and Yule in the north. Many of these festivals had religious overtones as believers attributed the promise of new life to their various gods. Early Christian leaders eventually adopted December 25 to commemorate the birth of their own god.

There is something magical about the passing of winter and the promise of spring; it's no surprise humans have always found reasons to celebrate this time of year. Whether we celebrate December 25 as a natural wonder, a secular festival or through religious observance, humans will likely continue celebrating "Christmas" for millennia to come.

Winter Solstice

For early civilizations, winter solstice marked a reversal of the sun's waning presence in the sky and a promise that spring would arrive after the long winter. This was an important promise to ancient peoples, and they viewed the shortest day of the year with mysticism. In fact, some of this planet's most impressive archeological sites, such as Britain's Stonehenge, align with the sun's rise and set on winter solstice. Winter solstice signaled that a time would come when plants and crops could grow again. To ancient civilizations, this was a reason to celebrate.

What is Winter Solstice?

The winter solstice is the shortest day of the year and the time at which the Sun is at its lowest point above the horizon. For sixth months after the winter solstice, each day has more sunshine than the last, bringing hope in the heart of winter and the promise of new life. This illustration shows the path of the sun in the sky on winter solstice, the shortest day of the year, and summer solstice, the longest day of the year.

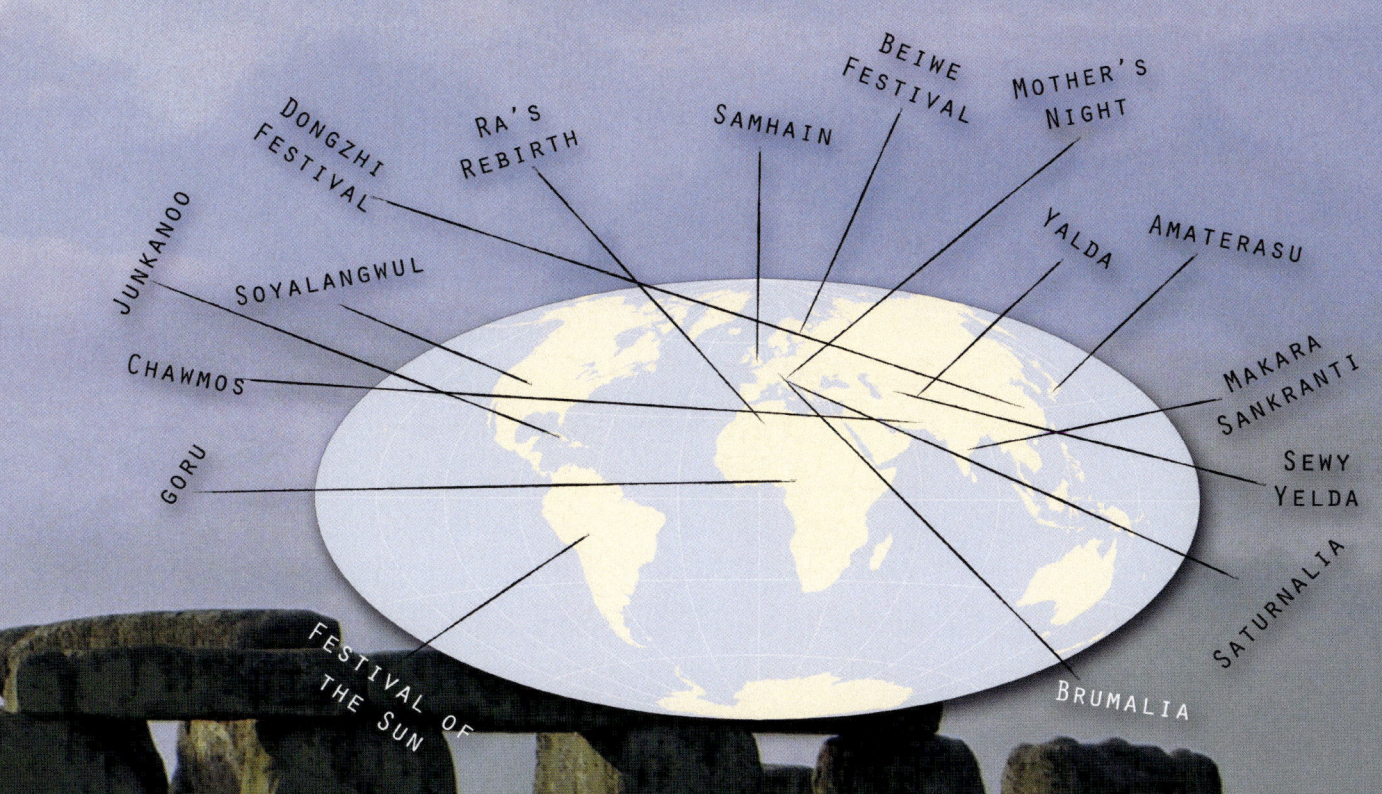

And celebrate they did! In Scandinavia people enjoyed Yule, and further south early Germans observed Mōdraniht, or Mothers' Night. The Celts of Western Europe celebrated midwinter and, in the south of modern England, Mummer's Day or Montol, which involved wearing disguises and engaging in raucous behavior. To the east, Persians celebrated winter solstice with Yalda, a holiday commemorating the victory of light and goodness over darkness and evil. The ancient Japanese winter solstice honored the return of sunlight to the world, and in the jungles of Peru and Bolivia ancient Incans welcomed winter solstice with the "Festival of the Sun." The Zuni and Hopi people of North America marked winter solstice with Soyalangwul, a ceremony to bring the sun back from its winter slumber.

Many of these ancient celebrations involved sun or agricultural gods. Ancient Babylonians held a festival at the winter solstice honoring the sun god Marduk's battle with darkness, similar to the Egyptians' midwinter celebration of their sun god, Ra. In Rome, believers honored Saturn, the god of agriculture, during wild winter solstice festivities. Since ancient times and throughout the world, celebrating the natural wonder of the winter solstice has been intertwined with supernatural mysticism.

Yule & Saturnalia

Most modern Christmas traditions trace their roots to one of two midwinter celebrations: Yule or Saturnalia. Yule developed in Northern Europe more than 2,000 years before Christ was born, in places where winter was dark and cold. The traditions of Yule - including enjoying warm drinks, brightening the night with candles and Yule logs, and decorating with mistletoe, evergreen and wheat stalks - reflect a society where winter solstice and the upcoming spring represented a promise of new life.

In the warmer south of Europe, winter solstice celebrations were less ritual and more carnival. Many Romans enjoyed Saturnalia, a holiday in honor of Saturn, the god of agriculture. Beginning the week before winter solstice and continuing for a full month, Saturnalia was a hedonistic time when food and drink were plentiful and the traditional Roman social order was upended. For a month, businesses and schools closed, slaves behaved like masters, and peasants poked fun at their leaders through mock government. It was a jolly time filled with good cheer.

Saturn, the God of Time and Harvest

In ancient Roman religion and myth, Saturn was a god of agriculture, liberation, and time. His reign was depicted as a Golden Age of abundance and peace. He was also a god of wealth, and the Temple of Saturn in the Roman Forum housed the state treasury. He was honored during Saturnalia, a time of feasting, role reversals, free speech, gift-giving and revelry. Saturn the planet and Saturday are both named after the god.

Ancient Romans, particularly the aristocracy and military near the time of Christ, also celebrated a winter solstice holiday honoring the god of light and harvest. *Dies Natalis Solis Invicti*, "the birthday of the unconquered sun," honored the infant Mithras, whose mythology shares much in common with that of Jesus Christ and whose worship predates Christianity by many centuries. Romans celebrated *Dies Natalis Solis Invicti* with special meals, singing, gift giving, and green decorations.

Because of the numerous winter solstice celebrations throughout Europe, early Christian leaders had a rich tableau of traditions and beliefs that could be incorporated into the celebration of Christ's birthday on December 25 ... whether they wanted them or not!

This very early Persian artwork shows Mithra as a giant sun disk being drawn across the sky in a chariot. Mithra was worshipped by many different cultures in various inincarnations for hunreds if not thousands of years before the birth of Christ. Early Christian leaders, noting the similarities between Christian and Mithraic mythology, argued that the Roman story of Mithra was a satanic lie meant to confuse early Christians.

PUTTING CHRIST IN CHRISTMAS

Jesus' birth is mentioned in only two of the four Biblical histories of Jesus' life, and his date of birth is not recorded anywhere. According to the account of Jesus' life written by his Disciple Luke, Jesus was probably born in the spring, at a time when shepherds were in the fields tending their flocks:

> And there were shepherds living out in the fields nearby, keeping watch over their flocks at night . . . "Today in the town of David, a Savior has been born to you; he is Christ the Lord."
>
> Luke 2:8, 11

But approximately 400 years after Jesus' death, in an attempt to promote Christianity and stamp out traditional celebrations, Pope Julius I chose to commemorate Jesus' birth on December 25, near the winter solstice and the dates of many religious festivals across the globe. These included *Dies Natalis Solis Invicti*, which reached the height of its popularity even as Christianity was becoming a major religion throughout the Roman Empire.

By celebrating Christmas at the same time as *Dies Natalis Solis Invicti*, Saturnalia, Yule and other traditional and pagan winter festivals, early Christian leaders made it more likely that Christmas would be embraced. First called the Feast of the Nativity, Christmas spread to Egypt by 432 A.D. and was being celebrated in England by the sixth century. Two hundred years later, Christmas was celebrated as far north as Scandinavia, where the words "Christmas" and "Yule" are synonyms to this day.

The Lord of Misrule

In England, the Lord of Misrule — known in Scotland as the Abbot of Unreason and in France as the Prince des Sots — was appointed by lot at Christmas to preside over a holiday feast. The Lord of Misrule was generally a peasant in charge of Christmas revelries, which often included drunkenness and wild partying, in the pagan tradition of Saturnalia.

The Lord of Misrule comes from antiquity. In ancient Rome, a Lord of Misrule was appointed for the feast of Saturnalia, in the guise of the good god Saturn. During this time, the ordinary rules of life were subverted as masters served their slaves, and the offices of state were held by slaves. The Lord of Misrule presided over all of this, and had the power to command anyone to do anything during the holiday period.

from Wikipedia, the free online encyclopedia

Early Christians knew that celebrating Christmas on the same day as traditional and pagan winter festivals would make the holiday more popular. But they didn't suspect that many of the customs and traditions of those pagan festivals would also become part of Christmas. Because of its festival roots, early Christmas celebrations were a boisterous mix of Christian themes and Saturnalian revelry. For example, a prominent component of Christmas during the middle ages was "Misrule," a time when ordinary rules were reversed. During Christmas Misrule, citizens would engage in all sorts of behavior that would be unacceptable during the year. The tradition of Misrule can be traced to Roman Saturnalia and was popular well into the 19th century. Today, Misrule is reflected in the tradition of Christmas crackers, which usually reveal a joke or a charm and the paper crown of the Lord of Misrule.

Christmas in America

It's hard not to celebrate Christmas in modern America. Nearly every facet of American social life is affected by the Christmas season as homes, businesses, schools and cities are transformed between Thanksgiving and New Year's Day. Americans who choose not to celebrate Christmas, whether for religious, social or other reasons, are labeled "Grinches" or "Scrooges." They may find themselves ostracized by strangers and criticized by friends. But this wasn't always the case.

In fact, many early Americans did not celebrate Christmas. Puritan immigrants saw Christmas as a symbol of decadence and paganism. They refused to celebrate Christmas and, at least in Boston, the holiday was outlawed from 1659 to 1681. The fine for showing Christmas spirit on the streets of Boston was five shillings! Although Christmas persisted in some early American communities, many U.S. citizens abandoned the English holiday after the American Revolution. For many generations, Christmas was celebrated as a minor holiday or not at all.

Christmas in Plymouth

Puritans believed all good practices come from the literal text of the Bible, and the Puritan community found no justification in the Bible to celebrate Christmas. They found Christmas especially troubling because they (correctly) believed its traditions were influenced by paganism. Christmas was illegal for a time in the Plymouth colony and Puritans continued to discourage Christmas celebrations even after they became legal.

This began to change in the 19th century as a Saturnalian Christmas spirit emerged in the form of civil unrest. In New York City, the city council established the city's first police force in the wake of a Christmas riot. As a backlash to disorderly Christmas revelry, some Americans began promoting Christmas as a season of charity and community spirit, rather than one of boisterous festivities. Several important books fostered this view of Christmas. For example, in 1819, best-selling American author Washington Irving wrote a fictional account of a Christmas celebration in an English manor house. His story, The Sketchbook of Geoffrey Crayon, described Christmas as a time when groups of different social statuses were united during a peaceful holiday season. His story also included ancient customs, such as the crowning of a Lord of Misrule, which created a template for modern celebrations.

Even more influential than Irving's book was a story written by an Englishman named Charles Dickens. A Christmas Carol stressed the importance of charity and goodwill by and towards all people. The book resonated with readers and changed how many Americans viewed the holiday season. As immigration to the United States skyrocketed during the late 19th and early 20th centuries, Americans rediscovered a hodgepodge of old Christmas traditions. Christmas was declared a federal holiday on June 26, 1870.

Most Americans today believe they celebrate Christmas in the same way it's always been enjoyed. But today's holiday season is really a mix of ancient traditions repurposed for the modern age. In fact, Christmas as we know it is scarcely 150 years old!

SANTA CLAUS

There is no Christmas symbol more beloved than the red suit and rosy cheeks of Santa Claus. The Santa Claus myth traces its origins to the Middle East, just a few centuries after Jesus' birth. In what is modern day Turkey, a man named Nicholas once traveled the countryside and used his inheritance to buy gifts for the poor and needy. Later canonized as St. Nicholas, he became the patron saint of children and his generosity has been an inspiration to Christians across millennia.

In the middle ages, countries across Europe celebrated the name day of St. Nicholas on December 6. In certain parts of Europe, children would be visited during that special night by Sinterklaas, who would bring gifts. Sinterklaas rode a white-grey horse through the sky and delivered his gifts through chimneys. His tiny helpers also carried a book that stated whether children had been good or bad during the previous year. In northern Europe, Sinterklaas replaced the pagan figure of Odin, who rode through the sky during winter solstice on his gray, eight-legged horse and entered houses through their chimneys.

In the 17th century, a separate holiday figure became popular in Britain. Father Christmas was notable for his wide girth, full beard and jolly disposition. He was frequently portrayed in a green, fur-lined cloak and was popularized internationally in Charles Dickens' A Christmas Carol as the Ghost of Christmas Present.

In the United States, the European Sinterklaas and British Father Christmas merged into a unique American figure: Santa Claus. In the early 19th century, the book A New-year's Present, to the Little Ones from Five to Twelve contained a poem describing "Old Santeclaus" as an old man on a reindeer sled who brought presents to children on Christmas Eve. At around the same time, a British minister wrote a poem based on the story of Nicholas: An Account of a Visit from St. Nicholas. Clement Clark Moore's story of St. Nick became world-famous:

> 'Twas the night before Christmas,
> when all through the house
> Not a creature was stirring, not even a mouse;
> The storckings were hung by the chimney with care
> In hopes that St. Nicholas soon would be there...

His poem describes the plump and jolly St. Nick and, for the first time, names eight reindeer pulling Santa's sleigh: Dasher, Dancer, Prancer, Vixen, Comet, Cupid, Donner and Blitzen. These and other popular stories captured the imaginations of boys and girls across the country, giving shape to the modern image of Santa.

In 1866, cartoonist Thomas Nast used his considerable talents to create images of Santa Claus to match the mysterious figure described in American poems and stories. The following decades fleshed out the Santa Claus story, including the 1869 story Santa Claus and His Works that identified Santa's home as the North Pole, a series of stories in the mid-19th century describing Mrs. Claus, and the beloved 1939 poem by Robert May, Rudolf the Red Nose Reindeer, later immortalized in a song with the same name by Gene Autry.

CHRISTMAS TREES

There is something special about the evergreen, a tree that maintains its beauty and dignity during even the coldest winter, that inspires humans. That may be why, from Egypt to Scandinavia to Scotland to America and across thousands of years, the evergreen tree has remained a powerful religious symbol of new life.

On winter solstice, residents of many northern European countries would hang cuttings or boughs of evergreen trees over their doors to ward away witches, ghosts, evil spirits, illnesses or other blights they believed to have a supernatural cause. The druids, Celtic holy men of northwestern Europe, decorated their temples with evergreen cuttings as symbols of everlasting life. Other ancient cultures, like the Egyptians, filled their homes with green palm rushes around the winter solstice to symbolize their sun god's triumph over death. The Vikings associated evergreens with their sun good, Balder.

The Christmas tree as we know it today is thought to have originated in Germany more than 400 years ago, when Christian believers began to bring trees into their homes and decorate them. Some scholars believe Martin Luther, the father of many modern-day Christian denominations, was the first to decorate his tree with lights to remind him of stars twinkling in the night (though he used candles instead of electric lights!).

Although the Christmas tree traveled to America in the 1700s with German settlers in Pennsylvania and elsewhere, it took many years to catch on with other residents of the New World. That was partly because many early Americans viewed the Christmas tree as a symbol of pagan beliefs – which, after all, it was! Some early American leaders worked hard to stamp out the Christmas tree and other pagan traditions that today are very important parts of our Christmas culture.

The Christmas tree was not fully adopted by Americans until the mid-19th century, and by the 1890s Christmas tree decorations were being imported from Germany to feed our decorating frenzy. While Europeans preferred small trees, Americans were recognized for erecting Christmas trees that filled up their entire rooms from floor to ceiling. By the early 20th century, Christmas trees were an important part of Americans' holiday celebrations both individually and as a community. The most famous Christmas tree in America, lit each year at Rockefeller Square in New York City, was first

GIVING GIFTS

Although Santa Claus only recently began giving gifts to good boys and girls, gift giving between families and strangers has been part of holiday traditions for thousands of years. During Saturnalia, ancient Romans exchanged simple gifts such as wax candles and pottery figures. Further north, mid-winter Yule celebrations included gift baskets made from wheat stalks and other symbols of life and fertility. But when Christians adopted December 25 as Jesus' birthday, church officials discouraged gift giving. At one point, the Catholic Church banned gift giving altogether.

But despite the church's edicts, the practice remained popular among Christians and pagans alike. Eventually the Christian church found an alternative: it adopted gift giving as its own. In the middle ages, the Catholic Church incorporated gift giving into the Christmas holiday to reflect the gifts of the Magi, who, according to the Bible, brought gifts of gold, frankincense and myrrh to the infant Jesus on the night of his birth. Christians also embraced the figure of St. Nicholas, known for giving gifts to the poor and needy. In one St. Nicholas story, he saved three daughters from an evil fate by dropping three bags of gold down their chimney. The bags landed in stockings hung by the fireplace to dry, just as modern children hang stockings from their mantles to receive Christmas goodies.

The modern gift giving tradition took root in Victorian England. The Victorians enjoyed Christmas as a time of family. charity and kindness, which were all embodied by gift-giving. At the same time, the industrial revolution slowly replaced traditional homemade gifts with manufactured goods. By the early 20th century, metal trains and factory-made dolls were common gifts. With the advent of the advertising age, Christmas gift giving transformed from the simple exchanges of Yule and Saturnalia into the commercial extravaganza we enjoy today.

Music & Carols

Nothing spreads holiday cheer like Christmas music, and no music moreso than traditional Christmas caroling. This winter tradition, during which carolers walk door-to-door to serenade friends and neighbors, is thousands of years old. The modern Christmas carol is descended from several ancient traditions, including Koleda, but is linked most directly to the wassail. For centuries in Europe, the wassail took place on the twelfth night of Christmas, when the spirit of Misrule and Saturnalian revelry reigned. During this night, wassailers – generally peasants – would visit their feudal lords and sing carols. In exchange for their music and goodwill, the lord of the manor would give food and drink to the wassailers. In later years, wassailers would visit wealthy neighbors in lieu of their lords.

Of course, wassailing had a dark side. In parts of England, groups of loud young men would threaten wealthy neighbors and demand free food and drink while wassailing. If they didn't get what they wanted, the men would curse their neighbor or vandalize his home. That's the origin of the famous wassail lyrics, "Give us some figgy pudding / we won't go until we get some."

Today, carolers enjoy singing secular wassails alongside true Christmas carols, which are religious hymns for the Christmas season. Many of the true carols we know today, including Silent Night, Joy to the World, The First Noel, God Rest Ye Merry Gentlemen, Good King Wenceslas, It came Upon a Midnight Clear and Hark the Herald Angels Sing, were written in the 18th and 19th centuries. Although the first known collection of Christmas carols was compiled by a chaplain named John Awdlay in 1426, carols were not sung regularly in churches until more than 400 years later. Just like many of the traditions described in this book, the modern Christmas carol has a long pedigree but is a relatively recent invention.

Multiple Choice

Reading for detail and comprehension.

1. In what city was Christmas spirit illegal during part of the 17th century?
    a. Boston
    b. New Amsterdam
    c. Plymouth
    d. Roanoke

2. Martin Luther added lights to his Christmas tree to remind him of:
    a. Street lamps.
    b. Fireflies.
    c. Stars.
    d. The light of Jesus Christ.

3. The winter solstice is:
    a. The first day of the solar calendar.
    b. The last day of the solar calendar.
    c. The shortest day of the year.
    d. The longest day of the year.

4. People have been singing Christmas carols in church regularly since:
    a. 1426
    b. The 16th century
    c. The 17th century
    d. The 19th century

5. Like the Norse god Odin, Sinterklaas rode through the sky on a horse and:
    a. Wore a great green cape.
    b. Entered homes through chimneys.
    c. Was accompanied by elves.
    d. Delivered gifts to good children.

6. Early Christians gave gifts at Christmas to symbolize:
    a. The Lord of Misrule.
    b. The Christmas spirit.
    c. The gifts of the Magi.
    d. The wassail.

7. The Evergreen tree is a symbol of:
    a. New life.
    b. Spring.
    c. Renewal.
    d. All of the above.

8. Homeowners who refused to give wassailers food and drink might be:
    a. Cursed.
    b. Vandalized.
    c. Both (a) and (b)
    d. None of the above.

9. Dies Natalis Solis Invicti occurred on December 25 and celebrated the birth of:
   a. Ra
   b. Mithras
   c. Jesus
   d. Saturn

10. Christmas has been celebrated since:
    a. Approximately the 3rd century A.D.
    b. The beginning of the Roman Empire.
    c. Approximately 3000 B.C.E.
    d. Throughout all recorded and archeological history.

11. Christmas is celebrated on December 25 because:
    a. Christians believed winter solstice had spiritual significance.
    b. Census records showed that Jesus was born on or around the end of December.
    c. According to the Bible, December 25 is the date of Jesus' birth.
    d. December 25 coincided with pre-existing religious festivals and celebrations.

12. The winter solstice has been celebrated since:
    a. Approximately the 3rd century A.D.
    b. The beginning of the Roman Empire.
    c. Approximately 3000 B.C.E.
    d. Throughout all recorded and archeological history.

13. These two books helped to popularize Christmas in the United States:
    a. The Sketchbook of Geoffrey Crayon and A Christmas Carol
    b. The Sketchbook of Geoffrey Crayon and Tales of Christmas
    c. Tales of Christmas and A Christmas Carol
    d. Tales of Christmas and An Account of a Visit from St. Nicholas

1. (A), 2. (C), 3. (C), 4. (C), 5. (b), 6. (C), 7. (D), 8. (C), 9. (B), 10. (A), 11. (D), 12. (D), 13. (A)

Short Answer

Thinking Critically.

Do you celebrate Christmas? Why or why not?

Describe your family's Christmas or winter holiday traditions. How did those traditions begin? How have they changed over time? Talk to your parents or grandparents to learn more about your family's traditions.

What are some American Christmas traditions not discussed in this book that have developed in just the past 50 years?

During the past 1,700 years, Christmas has transformed from a simple religious feast to a boisterous carnival to a family celebration to a commercial extravaganza. How do you think Christmas will evolve next? How will modern culture will affect that change?

In an attempt to make Christmas more popular, early Christian leaders scheduled Christmas on December 25 to coincide with other religious celebrations. Do you think this approach would work today for new holidays? What new holidays have developed in the past 50 years around the Christmas season?

Does understanding why and how Christmas traditions develop make them feel more or less valuable to you? Why?

LONG ANSWER

Applying Research & Writing Skills

There are many Christmas traditions not discussed in this book. Research these modern Christmas traditions and write a short history about each:

- Christmas Lights
- Santa's Reindeer
- Holiday Cards
- Snowmen
- Fruitcakes

The winter holiday "Festivus" is celebrated each year on December 23. Research Festivus, and imagine a future 200 years from now when Christmas and Festivus traditions have merged into a single holiday. Write a story about a Christmas-Festivus meal during this new holiday season. Describe the new holiday and its traditions.

Do people still celebrate winter solstice? If so, describe their winter solstice holiday traditions. What similarities are there between pagan winter solstice traditions and modern Christmas traditions?

Made in the USA
Columbia, SC
07 November 2019